The Duke of
WELLINGTON

WHO WAS...

The Duke of WELLINGTON

The Gentleman Soldier

JOSHUA DODER

Illustrations by Alex Fox

✶ SHORT BOOKS

First published in 2006 by
Short Books
3A Exmouth House
Pine Street
London EC1R 0JH

10 9 8 7 6 5 4 3 2 1

Copyright ©
Joshua Doder 2006

Joshua Doder has asserted his right under the Copyright,
Designs and Patents Act 1988 to be identified as the
author of this work. All rights reserved. No part of this
publication may be reproduced, stored in a retrieval
system or transmitted in any form, or by any means
(electronic, mechanical, or otherwise) without
the prior written permission of both the copyright
owners and the publisher.

A CIP catalogue record for this book
is available from the British Library.

Illustration copyright © Alex Fox 2006
Quiz copyright © Sebastian Blake 2006

ISBN 1-904977-62-6

Printed in Great Britain by
Bookmarque Ltd., Croydon, Surrey

PROLOGUE

A hundred thousand men are waiting to die. On a field in Belgium, they eat their breakfast, pack their bags and clean their guns.

It is early in the morning. The birds are singing. The rain has slowed to a light drizzle, and the sun is shining through the clouds.

A tall, thin man looks across the landscape. He stares at the smoke and the colours, the cannons and the men. He knows that, by the end of the day, he might be acclaimed as the greatest soldier that Britain has ever produced. Or he will be humiliated.

Living or dying doesn't matter to him. What matters is winning.

His name is Arthur. His official title is the Duke of Wellington. His soldiers call him Nosey.

For twenty years, he has been waiting for today. For twenty years, he has been fighting against the armies of Napoleon Bonaparte. But he and Napoleon have never stood on opposite sides of the same battlefield. They have never fought one another in person.

By the end of the day, one of them will be destroyed. Many great soldiers die during their greatest triumphs. If Arthur has to die in order to win, then he will die happily. And if he has not won the battle, he would rather be dead than alive.

He glances down at the map in his hands, then snaps his fingers at another officer.

The officer hurries towards him, carrying a telescope.

Arthur lifts the telescope to his eye. He stares across the fields, trying to pick out the separate regiments. He wants to see all the different groups of men under his command.

Through the telescope, he stares across the field at the French Army. They are close enough to see clearly. Just like Arthur's soldiers, they have spent the past hour eating their breakfast, packing their bags and cleaning their guns. Yesterday's terrible thunderstorm has turned into a slow, steady drizzle. The ground is soft and muddy. The men are wet and cold.

Even the horses are shivering.

Soon, all these men will say a few final words to their friends. They will wish one another "good luck". They will shake hands. They will think about their wives and their girlfriends, their parents and their children. They will take a deep breath, and wait for their signal. And when they hear the whistle or the shout, they will march into battle.

Nothing makes a noise like that – the noise of men fighting for their lives. Thousands and thousands of men, hoping to live, trying to kill. There is no noise so noble, so exciting and so terrifying.

It is a noise that Arthur knows very well.

Through the telescope, he searches the opposite side of the field, and tries to see his opponent.

Napoleon.

Somewhere over there, on the opposite side of the field, Napoleon will be standing with his officers, staring through a telescope of his own. He will be looking at his troops, picking out the different regiments, and casting his eye over the enemy, hoping to find weak spots and deciding where to attack.

The two of them are probably staring at one another now.

Arthur smiles. He snaps shut his telescope, and turns around. It is time to begin. It is time to fight the greatest battle of his life.

CHAPTER ONE

In the summer of 1769, two babies were born a thousand miles apart.

At the beginning of the summer, in the cool rains of May, a boy was born in Dublin, the capital of Ireland. He was christened Arthur.

At the end of the summer, in the brutal heat of August, a boy was born in Ajaccio, the capital of Corsica. He was christened Napoleon.

Forty-six years later, these two boys would meet and fight at the Battle of Waterloo. But in the summer of 1769, they just lay in their cots, a thousand miles apart, and screamed and yelled and waved their little fists in the air until they were given some milk.

This book will tell the story of one of those babies.

Over the course of his life, he was called Arthur

Wesley, Arthur Wellesley, the Duke of Wellington, Nosey and the Iron Duke.

His full title at the end of his life was Field Marshal the Most Noble Arthur Wellesley, Duke of Wellington, Marquess of Wellington, Marquess Douro, Earl of Wellington, Viscount Wellington of Talavera and of Wellington, Baron Douro of Wellesley, Prince of Waterloo, Duke of Brunoy, Duke of Vittoria, Marquis of Torres Vedras, Conde de Vimiero, Duke of Ciudad Rodrigo, Grandee of the First Class, Knight of the Garter, Knight of St Patrick, Knight Grand Cross of the Bath, Knight of the Golden Fleece, Knight Grand Cross of Hanover, Knight of the Sword of Sweden, Knight of the Annunciado of Sardinia, Knight of St Andrew of Russia, Knight of St George of Russia, Knight of Maria Teresa, Knight of the Crown of Rue Saxony, Knight of St Hermenegilda of Spain, Knight of the Red Eagle of Brandenburg, Knight of the Golden Lion of Hesse-Kassel, Lord of the Privy Council, Fellow of the Royal Society.

But I'm going to call him Arthur.

Arthur was born on May 1 1769. His father was Garret Wesley, First Earl of Mornington. His mother was Anne Hill, Countess of Mornington.

His family originally came from Wells, a small,

elegant town in Somerset. They took their name from the town: Wells became Wesley or Wellesley. (They could never quite decide how to spell their name, and different members of the family spelled it in different ways.) The family moved from Somerset to Ireland, and lived in Dublin. Arthur's father, Garret Wesley, was always penniless. He adored music, and spent most of his time playing the violin or singing or composing little ditties. He wasn't interested in working.

Garret and Anne had five sons and a daughter. Arthur was the third son. His two elder brothers, Richard and William, were generally regarded as the clever members of the family. Arthur was the stupid one. He was quiet, everybody thought, and a bit useless. No-one ever believed that he would do anything with his life. Like his dad, he spent most of time playing the violin or staring out of the window, dreaming.

When Arthur was twelve, his father died and his mother sent all her sons to Eton – a posh boarding-school near Windsor. There, Arthur was utterly miserable.

His eldest brother Richard had already been at Eton for three years, and won several prizes for his brilliant command of Greek and Latin. No-one expected Arthur to do so well. And he didn't. At the large, violent school, he was always unhappy. He learnt only two useful lessons: how to fight with his fists and how to hide his feelings. But he did very badly in Greek, Latin, maths, history and all his other school subjects. He did so badly, in fact, that his mother decided to remove him from the school. Eton was extremely expensive and there didn't seem much point paying high fees to educate such a lazy, stupid boy. Arthur was sent to stay in Brighton, where he was taught privately by a tutor. That was no more successful, so Arthur moved from Brighton to Belgium, and lived there with his mother. In Belgium, he did at least learn how to speak perfect French – although with a strong Belgian accent. He also continued playing the violin quite nicely.

Looking at her hopeless son, Arthur's mother shook her head. What was going to become of him? An amateur violinist who spoke French with a Belgian accent – what use was he to anyone?

By the time that Arthur was seventeen, there didn't seem much point staying at school any longer. He never did anything except play the violin, and he could do that just as well at home. So his mother removed him from school and sent him to the Military Academy at Angers in France. There, he learnt the basics of soldiering.

He learnt how to fight with a sword. How to ride a horse into battle. How to build fortifications. How to command an army.

Finally, Arthur had found something that he could do well.

CHAPTER TWO

One evening in 1786, Arthur's mother went to the theatre in London. She looked across the audience, and saw a tall, handsome young man. Staring at him in amazement, she said, "I do believe there is my ugly boy Arthur." Her son had returned to London without telling her – and he had changed. The shy, awkward, useless boy had become a confident, handsome young man.

From London, Arthur went back to Ireland. He joined the army. And then family connections got him elected to Parliament. He had a pleasant life. He read lots of books, went to lots of parties, ate well, drank well, and rode horses every day. He also fell in love.

Everyone called her Kitty, although her full name was Lady Catherine Dorothea Sarah Pakenham. She was a short, thin girl who spent most of her time reading. Arthur asked her to marry him. Like any well brought-up girl, Kitty asked her mother and father what to do. They took a long look at the dreamy young soldier, who had no money and no prospects, and didn't seem to do anything with his life except stare out of the window and play the violin. Mr and Mrs Pakenham shook their heads. Following strict instructions from her parents, Kitty told Arthur that she could not marry him.

There were lots of other girls in Dublin. Arthur could have married one of them instead. But he wasn't the type of man who fell in and out of love easily and he decided that, one day, he would come back to Dublin, and Kitty Pakenham would marry him. One day...

But there were other things to do first. Over the Channel, a revolution was sweeping across France. The French were demanding *"liberté, égalité, fraternité, ou la mort"* – liberty, equality, brotherhood, or death. The French king lost his head and a republic was declared. Hundreds of French aristocrats were guillotined. And in 1793, France declared war on England.

This was a huge moment in Arthur's life. He had to make a choice. Either he could stay in Ireland, eating and drinking and riding horses and playing the violin and having a jolly nice time. Even if Kitty didn't want to marry him, some other girl would – his life would be easy and pleasant. Or he could work – and work so hard that, one day, Kitty's parents would allow her to say yes to him.

Arthur took his violin to the woods outside Dublin and gathered some twigs and sticks. He built a bonfire, and lit it. When the flames were blazing, he picked up his violin and plucked the strings for one last time. Then he leant down and thrust the violin into the flames. The varnish crackled. The wood burnt. Within minutes, the violin had been reduced to ash.

Arthur turned away from the ashes and hurried back to the city. He re-joined his fellow soldiers and boarded a boat. He was never to play the violin again.

Arthur spent several months in Holland and Belgium, fighting the French. It was cold, miserable and disastrous. The French won every battle. Arthur caught a terrible fever, and almost died. Years later, talking about these battles, Arthur said that he had learnt one very important lesson from those miserable months: he had learnt what not to do. And knowing what you should *not* do, said Arthur, is just as important as knowing what you *should* do.

In June 1796, his regiment received orders to stop fighting the French, and return to the port. They were to board their ships again, said the orders, and sail for India.

By now Arthur was twenty-eight years old. He had no money. He owed big debts. He had fallen in love with a beautiful woman who wouldn't marry him. He was a junior officer in the army, and he was being sent to fight on the other side of the world. In just about every way, his life looked hopeless. No-one would have believed that within a few years, he would be rich, married and one of the most famous men in Britain.

CHAPTER THREE

Arthur took five hundred books on the boat. But, apart from a few novels and some poetry, all the books were devoted to only two subjects: India and war. The voyage lasted eight months, so he had a lot of time for reading.

They left England in the early summer of 1796, crossed the Mediterranean, plodded down the coast of Africa, whizzed around the Cape of Good Hope and finally reached Calcutta in February 1797. During that time, Arthur had learnt everything that his books could teach about India and war. Now, it was time to put his reading into practice. Time to fight a war in India.

Calcutta was hot and sweaty. Arthur found somewhere to live, and unpacked his bags. He strolled through the streets in the company of British officers who had been living in India for many years. They told him about the local customs, advised him always to make friends with the beggars by giving them a few coins, and warned him not to eat any green chillis – not unless he wanted his mouth to explode.

Soon after Arthur arrived in India, a new Governer-General sailed to Calcutta, sent by the British government. His name was Richard Wellesley, and he was Arthur's elder brother. He brought another of their brothers, Henry, as his personal adviser. Arthur may have been living in a foreign country, thousands of miles from home, surrounded by peculiar people and bizarre food, but he was living among family and friends. Life wasn't too tough. If Arthur had been a different type of man, he would have sat back in a comfy chair, opened a bottle of wine, ordered a plate of curry and relaxed for a few months, to recover from his long voyage. Instead, he rolled up his sleeves and looked for a battle to fight.

He soon found one. The French had an ally in the south of India. His name was Tipu Sultan and he ruled a part of southern India called Mysore. (Today, the area has been renamed Karnataka). The French gave money and weapons to Tipu Sultan, and trained his troops. In return, he declared war on the British.

Tipu Sultan was a violent, brutal ruler. He loved danger and excitement, and his nickname was "the tiger". Here is one of the things that Tipu said about himself:

"I would rather live for two days like a tiger than two hundred years like a sheep."

Tipu was so proud of his ferocious reputation that he had a wooden statue made for himself, showing a tiger lying on top of a British man. Many years later the statue was given to the Victorian and Albert Museum in London, and you can see it there today. The tiger's mouth is open; he is just about to eat the man. The statue has a mechanical organ hidden inside, containing a pair of bellows and thirty-six pipes, which could be activated to sound like a tiger roaring and a man screaming.

Arthur slowly made his way with the British army towards Tipu Sultan. First, he sailed from Calcutta down to Madras, a port in the south of India. From there, he marched west to Seringapatam (a city which is now called Srirangapatnam). There, Arthur was given his first proper military job by his bosses: to attack the city in the middle of the night. Unfortunately, he did not have the chance to spy out the land during daylight, and the attack was a complete disaster. His men got lost in a swamp; they were bombarded with rockets and missiles; Arthur was shot in the knee. Hobbling, he ordered the retreat.

Arthur slouched back to his headquarters. He felt terribly depressed. He had been humiliated by Tipu's men. Would he ever get another chance? Or would he be sent back to Calcutta, and his troops given to another commander?

From his failure to capture Seringapatam, Arthur learnt one very important lesson. Before you go into battle, he realised, you must always know exactly who and what you are attacking. You must either have excellent maps of the area, or pay good spies to tell you what they have seen, or you must spend a lot of time staring through a telescope and watching where your soldiers are going to be fighting.

It was not a lesson that Arthur could put into practice immediately. After his failure, he was temporarily removed from command of the British troops, and another man led the assault on Seringapatam, a grumpy Scotsman named General Baird.

Baird had been locked in one of Tipu Sultan's prisons for three years. He had been released in an exchange of prisoners. Now, he wanted the chance to take his revenge.

Drawing his sword and shouting at his men, Baird led the army over the walls of Seringapatam and into the city. They were much more successful than Arthur had been. The Indian soldiers forgot their French training, dropped their guns, and fled. The British swarmed over the walls and took control of the city.

General Baird ran through the streets, searching for Tipu Sultan. All he wanted was to find the man who had imprisoned him. He couldn't get those three years back again – but he could make Tipu suffer for them.

Finally, Baird discovered Tipu lying on a mattress, surrounded by his servants. But there was no chance for Baird to take his revenge. Tipu had already been shot through the head by a British bullet.

***

With Tipu Sultan gone, the British looked around for another way to attack the French. Arthur pored over his maps and plotted to invade Mauritius, an island that lies in the middle of the ocean between India and Africa; but his superiors vetoed the plan. Then he caught a terrible disease which covered his body with an itchy red rash. There was only one way to get rid of the rash – he had to bathe in acid every day.

Arthur was thirty-one years old. He was thin, bored, lonely and lying in a bath of acid. Could things get any worse?

They could. A great job came up – fighting the French in Egypt – but General Baird was appointed to lead the army. While Baird sailed to Egypt, Arthur stayed in India. He was posted to Seringapatam and ordered to rule the city, making sure that none of the locals rebelled against the British.

Arthur had never been so bored in his life. There was nothing to do except play billiards, read books and hunt wild animals in the jungle. He spent as much time as possible riding through the countryside, watching the habits of the local people, seeing how they lived. Although he never learnt to speak any local languages, he did begin to understand the most basic words, and could tell when an interpreter had wrongly translated what he was trying to say. Arthur realised another vital lesson: if you're going to fight a war in a foreign country, you have to understand how the natives live. You have to know their habits. And, if possible, you have to persuade them to like you – or, at least, to respect you.

But he never got too friendly with the locals. He never allowed them to forget who was boss. Once, for instance, Arthur was dining with a Maharajah, one of the local rulers, who desperately wanted to know what the British were planning to do next. The Maharajah badgered Arthur with questions, asking about his tactics, his plans and his ambitions. Arthur refused to reply. Finally, Arthur leaned across the table and said in a low voice, "Can you keep a secret?"

"Yes, of course," the Maharajah replied eagerly.

Arthur nodded. "So can I."

Dinner parties, hunting in the jungle, chatting to the local nobility, flirting with the pretty girls – this was all very well, thought Arthur, but it wasn't what he wanted from life. He wanted to be fighting a good war. He wondered whether to request a transfer out of India and back to a country where some decent battles could be fought.

Just as Arthur was beginning to despair, the government gave him a new job: to destroy the French-trained armies that controlled the middle of India. Arthur summoned his soldiers and marched through the countryside, planning to knock out the enemy's fortresses one by one.

To his surprise, Arthur stumbled across his opponent much more quickly than he had expected. His own army was small – about seven thousand men – and lightly armed, pulling only a few cannons. Opposite him, he saw a huge force assembled around the little village of Assaye. There were forty or fifty thousand men, protected by more than a hundred cannons and a great herd of cavalry.

By talking to his spies, and staring at the enemy through his telescope, Arthur reached an uncomfortable realisation. For every British soldier on the battlefield, the Indians had seven. Even worse, the British were exhausted, having walked twenty miles already that day.

The British could not retreat, because they would be cut to pieces. Nor could they stay still: the cannons would slaughter them. They had only one option: to attack. But could every British soldier really fight seven Indians? How can you fight seven men at the same time?

It was the toughest test that Arthur had ever faced. He stood in the midst of his troops, staring at the landscape through his telescope, and listening to the advice of his spies and assistants.

"Don't attack," said one of them.

"Make peace," said another.

"Retreat," said a third.

"There is no way that you could possibly defeat such a big army," said a fourth. "Better to get away now."

The sun was hot. The air was so thick that you could hardly breathe. The British troops were exhausted. They faced an enemy who had more guns, more cannons, more horses and many more men.

Arthur smiled and said, "We shall attack." He gathered his officers, and described his plan. Then he led them into battle.

The British troops charged across the river. They

were knocked back by barrages of bullets. Cannonballs thumped into their bodies. The dust was soon wet with blood.

One of the men riding alongside Arthur suddenly had no head. A cannonball had hit him in the face. The headless man rode on for a few paces, blood spurting out of his neck, his horse bucking and whinnying in terror. Then the headless body slid to the ground and lay still.

Bullets peppered Arthur's horse. As the horse collapsed to the ground, Arthur jumped aside and ordered one of his fellow officers to dismount. "Thank you," said Arthur. "I shall return your horse later." Swinging himself up into the saddle, he grabbed the reins and rode into the battle. The officer, robbed of his horse, stood there for a minute, scratching his head, wondering if he would ever see his horse or Arthur again.

The battle was long and bloody. By the end of the day, a third of the British soldiers had been killed or wounded. But the Indians had fled.

That night, British soldiers roamed the battlefield, searching for loot. They picked coins and jewels from dead men's bodies, and pulled guns and knives from cold hands. Wounded men crawled across the dust, begging someone to give them a sip of water.

Arthur sat alone in his tent with his head in his hands. He thought about his friends who had been killed, and others who had been wounded – losing an arm or a leg. He remembered the pools of blood, soaking into the hot dust. As he had learned to always do after a battle, he thought through exactly what he had said and done during the long, hot day, and tried to decide what he could have done better.

You must remember that fighting a battle in the 1790s was very different to fighting a battle today. Arthur had none of the technological gizmos that modern soldiers use. His soldiers had very simple weapons. All the men carried swords, lances, daggers or bayonets. Their guns could only be fired once before they needed to be re-loaded. If a man was charging towards you, there would only be enough time to fire a single shot. If your shot missed, you would have to draw your sword and fight hand to hand.

Arthur's army had three sections. Firstly, there was the artillery: big guns that fired cannonballs which could smash into twenty or thirty men, leaving a trail of arms and legs. Secondly, there was the cavalry: men on horses charging across the battlefield, hacking the enemy with swords and lances. Thirdly, there was the largest and simplest part of the army: the infantry, who fought on foot.

Perhaps the most important difference between Arthur's army and modern armies is communication. A modern general always knows what is happening all over the battlefield. Using radios, he can talk to his officers – wherever they are. Using helicopters and planes, cameras and satellites, he can see the battlefield. He knows the position of his enemy – and, just as importantly, he knows the position of his own troops.

For Arthur, things were very different. He could see only with his eyes. He could issue orders only to men who were close enough to hear his voice. Most of the time, he didn't really know what was happening. People arrived, running or galloping on horseback, bringing news from different parts of the battlefield. Often, several people would arrive at the same time, each of them saying something completely different. Arthur would send them back again with his orders – "march to the north", for instance, or "attack now!" – but he could never be completely sure that his orders would actually reach the right people. If the messenger was shot by a stray bullet, the message would never arrive.

The best commanders were constantly moving across the battlefield, seeing what was happening, watching the enemy and giving orders. Above all, a great general would show his men that he had no fear. Bullets might be whizzing around his head. Cannonballs might be thumping into the ground by his feet. But he would take no notice. He would have more important things to think about.

Later in his life, Arthur was asked what had been the most difficult battle that he ever fought. "Assaye," he replied. Nothing ever compared to the heat, the exhaustion and the difficulty of being outnumbered seven to one.

In March 1805, nine years after he'd left home, Arthur boarded a boat and sailed back to England. They had been long and difficult years. He had been poisoned by all kinds of tropical diseases. He had been peppered by bullets from enemy guns. He had watched his soldiers die. He had been responsible for the deaths of many men, both British and Indian.

But he had achieved three very important things. Firstly, he had earned enough money to enable him to do whatever he wanted with his life. This meant he could buy a house. He could afford to keep servants and horses. He could get married.

Secondly, he had learnt how to be a good soldier. When he sailed to India, he had known about soldiering from books and blackboards. Now, he knew his profession from the real experience of preparing for a battle and engaging with the enemy. He could control men, issue orders and impose his wishes on a battlefield. He knew what it felt like to win and what it felt like to lose.

Thirdly, and most importantly, he had filled himself with confidence. After almost a decade abroad, working as a soldier, Arthur felt absolutely confident that he could fight anyone in the world. Give him a few good men, some clean guns, a map and a telescope, and he would win the battle.

Now, he was ready to fight any man on the planet. Even Napoleon.

CHAPTER FOUR

On the long voyage back to England, Arthur stopped at a small island in the Atlantic Ocean. He was delighted by the climate and the exceptional natural beauty of the place, and stayed for a month.

The island was called St Helena. Several years later, Napoleon would go there too – and stay in the same house where Arthur had stayed.

But that was more than ten years in the future. In 1805, Napoleon had no intention of sailing to St Helena. He was the most famous man in Europe, winning battle after battle, raging across the continent at the head of a victorious French army. Having already declared himself the Emperor of France, he had just been crowned King of Italy in Milan Cathedral. The world lay at his feet. He had probably never even heard of a British soldier named Arthur Wellesley. But he would soon.

After a month's holiday on St Helena, Arthur boarded another boat, and sailed across the ocean to England. He arrived home to discover that most of Europe had united against the French. Britain, Russia and Austria had signed a treaty, promising to support one another and destroy Napoleon.

To his intense irritation, Arthur couldn't find an active job with the army. He was posted to a brigade in Sussex. He marched up the hills with his men. Then he marched them down again. When they had finished marching up and down, they cleaned their guns and polished their boots. It was fabulously boring.

One afternoon, Arthur sat down at his desk and wrote a letter to Kitty Pakenham.

They had not met for more than ten years. While he had been travelling around the world, she had been living peacefully in Ireland. During all those years, they had never written to one another. Through mutual friends, they had heard a little about one another's lives, but never made any attempt to stay in contact. Nevertheless, Arthur wrote to Kitty and asked if she would like to marry him.

A few days, Kitty wrote back, saying, "Yes, I will." Then she wrote a few more words: "But do you not think we should meet first?"

"We shall meet soon," replied Arthur.

So, it was settled. They would get married. But they still had not met – and, to everyone's surprise, Arthur showed no enthusiam for travelling to Ireland and seeing his fiancée. You might have thought that he would jump onto the first boat sailing from Bristol or Liverpool, and rush to meet Kitty in Dublin. But he kept finding vital reasons to stay in London. He had important meetings with politicians. He had dinners with soldiers. He wrote long articles on the military situation in India. He sailed to Germany, took one look at the place, and sailed straight back home again. Finally, six months after they had agreed to marry, Arthur found time to travel across the sea to Ireland to see Kitty for the first time in ten years.

He was not very pleased by what he found. Entering her house and spotting her at the other end of the drawing-room, he didn't gasp in joy or sprint to grab her hand. Instead, he turned to one of his friends and whispered, "By Jove, she has grown ugly!"

But Arthur was not the type of man who changed his mind about things. He had always wanted to marry Kitty, so he would marry her, even if he didn't much like the look of her. Even if she had developed from a lively, exciting girl into an anxious, unattractive woman. He took a deep breath, strode across the room, and greeted her. "Hello, my dear," he said.

Kitty glanced nervously at him. "Hello, Arthur," she replied in a quiet voice.

They smiled at one another, but neither of them could think of anything else to say.

In the time that they had spent apart, both of them had changed. Arthur now looked taller, thinner and much more authoritative. His skin had been burnt by the hot Indian sun. Most of his hair had gone – as had all his shyness.

Kitty seemed to have shrunk. She had grown thinner and paler. Her good looks had faded and her jolly laughter and constant stream of jokes had been replaced by an nervous smile.

That night, they spoke awkwardly to one another. They had little to say. Arthur made a couple of witticisms. Kitty laughed politely. Each of them explained what they had done over the past ten years. They discussed Arthur's magnificent Indian victories and Kitty's quiet Irish life.

Anyone watching would have known that these two awkward people had little or nothing in common. However, Arthur and Kitty had made a solemn promise to marry one another, and they were not the type of people who broke their promises. So they got married.

After the wedding, they spent a week's honeymoon together, then moved to London. Immediately, Arthur devoted himself to finding a new job. All he wanted was another army to run, and another chance to fight the French.

Ten months after they married, Arthur and Kitty had their first child. He was a boy, and they named him Arthur Richard Wellesley. A year later, Kitty had another boy whom they called Charles.

While Arthur searched for work, Kitty was left alone to look after the house and take care of the two boys. She was sad and lonely. For both Arthur and Kitty, their marriage brought nothing but unhappiness.

Domestic life bored Arthur. His wife and children irritated him. He longed to be standing at the head of a group of men, smelling gunpowder and hearing the cries of horses, surrounded by maps and telescopes, preparing to march into battle.

His frustration increased as he watched the fabulous progress made by Napoleon in Europe. Rushing across the continent with his fearsome army, Napoleon defeated opponent after opponent. He seemed unstoppable. France was triumphant. Italy, Austria, Prussia, Denmark – one by one, they fell to Napoleon. Even Russia and Spain made treaties with the French. Only one country resisted the little Corsican. Only one country had an appetite for battle. The question was this: did Britain have an army and a general who could defeat France and Napoleon?

There was one piece of good news for the British. Napoleon had been too bold with the Spanish. He had removed the King of Spain from his throne and sent him into exile, and then Napoleon placed his own brother, Joseph Bonaparte, on the Spanish throne. The Spanish were furious. They rebelled, rioted and swore terrible revenge.

A group of Spaniards arrived in Britain, begging the British government to send an army to attack the

Bonaparte brothers. The British agreed. They asked Arthur to command the army. He accepted immediately, and started gathering men and provisions for the voyage.

Arthur was forty years old and his great chance had finally arrived.

CHAPTER FIVE

A few days before Arthur sailed to Portugal, he had dinner with John Wilson Croker, an Irish lawyer. In those days, the ladies would retire to the drawing-room after eating, and leave the men to drink port or brandy, smoke cigars and talk about manly things.

When Kitty left the room, Arthur fell silent. He gazed at the ceiling. For several minutes, not a word was spoken. Finally, John Wilson Croker cleared his throat, and said to his host, "What are you thinking about, sir?"

Arthur replied, "Well, to say the truth, I am thinking of the French that I am going to fight."

(John Wilson Croker kept notes of all his interesting conversations and published them in a book, *The Croker Papers*, which is how we now know exactly what Arthur said that night.)

Arthur continued, "I have not seen them since the campaign in Flanders, when they were capital soldiers; and a dozen years of victory under Bonaparte must have made them better still. Besides, they have a new system of strategy, it seems, which has outmanoeuvred and overwhelmed all the armies of Europe. Tis enough to make one thoughtful; but no matter: my die is cast, they may overwhelm me, but I don't think they will outmanoeuvre me. First, because I am not afraid of them, as everybody else seems to be; and, secondly, because, if what I hear of their system of manoeuvres is true, I think it is a false one against steady troops. I suspect that all the continental armies were more than half beaten before the battle was begun – I, at least, will not be frightened beforehand."

The whole of Europe feared Napoleon and the French army – but not Arthur. He trusted his soldiers, and he had total confidence in his own abilities as their commander.

When Arthur arrived in Portugal, he discovered that the British government had betrayed him. Having promised that he could lead the army, they then gave the command to an older, more experienced soldier instead. Arthur was furious. Appalled by the behaviour of the old general, who negotiated a surrender with a group of defeated French troops – allowing them to return to France with all their loot – Arthur jumped on the first available ship and returned to England. If he couldn't run the army in his own way, he would rather stay at home.

***

Back in London, Arthur found himself wondering what to do with his life. But then he was saved by a piece of good luck. Two more old generals took turns to command the British army in Portugal. One by one, they were defeated or killed. The government came back to Arthur, and asked him again if he would take command of the army and, this time, he could run it in his own way. He accepted, and jumped aboard the fastest ship that he could find.

Arriving in Lisbon, Arthur found a party thrown in his honour. The citizens believed that he, and only he, would save them from the French. Dancers packed the streets. The women clicked castenets. The men strummed guitars. Banners hung from buildings, emblazoned with the slogan "Conquer or die!" Arthur smiled politely, walked straight past all the party-goers, and demanded to see his officers. He took no notice of the fine food, the delicious wine or the beautiful dancing women. Instead, he ordered his men to prepare for an immediate departure.

Arthur's first task was simple: he had to remove the French army from Portugal, and drive them back into Spain. Only two days after arriving in Lisbon, while most men would still have been recovering from the voyage and accustoming themselves to their new surroundings, Arthur marched out of the city at the head of his army. They went north.

In his army, Arthur had a mixture of British and Portuguese troops. Rather than keeping them apart, he jumbled the two nationalities together, so each could benefit from the other's presence. The Portuguese could learn some discipline from the British, thought Arthur, and the British could learn a few words of Portuguese.

The French army retreated to Oporto, a city that lay a couple of hundred miles up the coast from Lisbon, on the north bank of the River Douro. The British would be approaching from the south and if they couldn't cross the river, they wouldn't be able to reach the city.

The French army was commanded by Marshal Soult. He withdrew his men across the River Douro, and positioned them inside Oporto. He ordered his soldiers to hunt up and down the banks of the river, and destroy every boat that they could find. Finally, his engineers blew up all the bridges with dynamite. It was now impossible to cross the Douro. Confident that the British could not reach Oporto, Marshal Soult ordered his cook to prepare an excellent lunch for the following day. Then he went to bed.

Early the next morning, while Marshal Soult was

still snoozing, one of Arthur's officers hurried up and down the south bank of the River Douro. He was searching for a way to get across to the north bank. Just as he was about to give up, he found something. Hidden in the reeds, he discovered a small fishing-boat. It was only big enough to carry five or six men. He climbed aboard and, taking some locals with him – a barber, a shepherd and some fishermen – he sailed across the river. On the other bank, right underneath the walls of the town, they discovered three big barges. One by one, they sailed the barges back to the other side. The officer sent a message to Arthur, describing what he had done and asking a simple question. "What shall we do next?"

Arthur's reply came back immediately. "Attack!"

Unnoticed by the French, who were playing cards or dreaming about their lunch, the three barges raced back and forth across the Douro. Each barge carried thirty men. Arriving on the other bank, the British soldiers scrambled up the hill and occupied a large building. They lined up their guns through the windows, and waited for the order to shoot.

Finally, a French guard noticed what had happened. *"Mon Dieu!"* he screeched at the top of his voice and pointed at the red-jacketed men and their rifles. *"Les Anglais! Les Anglais!"* He ran through the town, shouting and whistling, warning his fellow soldiers to drop their cards, forget their lunches and pick up their guns.

But it was too late. Right under the noses of the French, six hundred British soldiers had crossed the river in fishing-boats and barges. Some of them peppered the French with bullets. Others swarmed through the gates and occupied the town.

Taken completely by surprise, the French had no time to fight. They didn't even have time to pack their bags. They fled out of Oporto and sprinted into the fields, leaving their luggage, their guns, their wounded and even their lunch.

As soon as Arthur entered the city, he hurried into Marshal Soult's lodgings, sat down at the table and ate the large, delicious meal which had been cooked for the French commander. Arthur wasn't usually very interested in food, and didn't particularly care what he ate. But this time, he savoured every mouthful.

After this success against the French, Arthur wrote, "The ball is now at my foot, and I hope I shall have strength enough to give it a good kick."

Unfortunately, he did not. He booted the French out of Portugal, but he could not remove them from Spain. He lacked sufficient support from his Spanish allies and could hardly afford to pay or feed his own troops. They were tired and hungry. The fields had been stripped of anything edible and the British government was too slow in providing supplies of food, drink and cash.

Marshal Soult regrouped his men, reinforced them with new guns and fresh ammunition, and drove the British back into Portugal. Arthur blamed the Spanish for his failure, and wrote to the Prime Minister: "I can only tell you that I feel no inclination to join in cooperation with them again."

***

Throughout that long, chilly winter, Arthur and his army stayed in Portugal. They never saw the French, although they did get one piece of nerve-wracking news: Napoleon had announced his intention to march down to Spain with a hundred and forty thousand of his best troops, and wipe out the British. Napoleon had finally heard of Arthur Wellesley – but he didn't yet think of him as a threat. More like an irritating little insect that was buzzing around, making a lot of noise, but could be brushed aside with one swipe of your hand.

Other men might have been scared by the thought of Napoleon and his armies. Not Arthur. Coolly and calmly, he prepared for the battles to come. He used that winter to construct a series of fortifications to protect Lisbon. He called them the lines of Torres Vedras. His men dug trenches and built fortresses, covering the landscape with an impregnable barrier – a long stone wall protected by hundreds of guns. He was sure that the lines of Torres Vedras would be enough to stop any army, however big and well-armed.

Arthur worked his men hard, allowing them little time off. He let his officers go on holiday – but only for twenty-four hours. That was enough time to amuse yourself, explained Arthur.

During the five years that Arthur spent in Portugal, he took no holiday at all. He never sailed back to Britain to see his wife and two sons, nor did he write them many letters. War was what interested Arthur. Not women or children.

He devoted almost his entire life to his work, so he expected his men to do the same. Arthur never slept for more than six hours a night, and often only three. He regularly forgot to eat. While his fellow officers feasted on roast meats and fine wines, Arthur was happy with some bread, a little cheese and a slice of ham. Sometimes, he would go out riding with a boiled egg in his pocket, and eat nothing else all day.

***

In the spring, the French returned with a bigger army – more than three times the size of Arthur's. Determined to flush the British out of Portugal, they crossed the border, and marched towards Lisbon. They moved quickly, sweeping across the landscape, driving the British before them, until they were stopped by a line of forts and walls built on the hills. It was the lines of Torres Vedras – the fortifications that Arthur had built. British and Portuguese soldiers peered through crevices. Cannons and rifles poked out of every gap.

The French hurled more and more men at the fortifications, but every attack was repulsed. Whenever a Frenchman came anywhere near the lines of Torres Vedras, he was greeted by whistling bullets and thudding cannonballs. Finally, the French had lost so many men and so much equipment that they could not continue. They turned around and retreated towards Spain.

Arthur's men poured down the hillsides and pursued the French. This time, Arthur was sure, he wouldn't just chase them out of Portugal, he would beat them back through Spain, into France and all the way to Paris.

CHAPTER SIX

Arthur charged across Spain with his army, pushing the French further and further towards the border. He beseiged Ciudad Rodrigo, then moved the army forward to the walled city of Badajoz.

The French waited behind the walls. Every day, the British attacked. Every night, the French rebuilt their defences. It was a long, brutal fight. The French put metal spikes in the ground, and rolled burning barrels down the slopes. Even to reach the walls, the British had to clamber across deep ditches. Soon, every ditch was filled with the bodies of dead and dying soldiers.

When the British finally reached the walls of Badajoz, they placed ladders against the bricks and started climbing – but the French leaned down from the walls with swords and axes, chopping the rungs, or dangled blazing torches to set fire to the wood. Every British ladder was smashed or burnt before a single man could get anywhere near the top of the wall.

The British made forty attacks. Forty times, they were beaten back. They walked over the bodies of their own dead friends and comrades.

The French soldiers stood on top of the walls, laughing and waving their arms, and shouted down: "What's wrong? Have you changed your mind? Have you decided you don't want to come in to Badajoz?"

Finally, on the forty-first attack, one British soldier

managed to climb one ladder, and leap over the top of the walls. That was enough. While he fought off the French troops, more men swarmed up the ladder behind him. They sprinted along the ramparts and poured into the town. The French turned and ran.

***

That night, when the battle had finished, Arthur walked along the smashed-up walls. He stared at the shattered corpses of his soldiers. Hundreds had died. He turned his face so no-one could see his eyes, but he wasn't quick enough. According to the officers who accompanied him, Arthur was weeping. The next day, when he read the long lists of all the dead men, he wept again.

That was one of the very few times that anyone saw Arthur showing any great emotion. It didn't last long. Two days after the siege had finished, while his men were still lying drunk in the streets, celebrating their victory, Arthur was hunched over his map, quietly and calmly planning the next stage of the campaign.

He marched fifty thousand men across Spain, and chased the French army up and down the countryside. Every morning, he forced his men to wake at four o'clock. They breakfasted on beer and onions, and spent the day marching. Finally, the two armies clashed at Salamanca.

Arthur was not one of those generals who watches war from a safe distance, avoiding all the bullets and hearing what has happened only through the reports of his officers. He insisted on seeing exactly what was happening. As bullets and cannonballs flew through the air, he rode on his horse, personally issuing orders to his men. He was often wounded, and several times he narrowly avoided being captured by the French. But his men knew that he faced the same dangers as them, and that made them trust him. "If Nosey is with us," they said to one another, "then we're going to win."

And they did. Salamanca was a great victory. At the end of the day, Arthur ordered his cavalry to charge. As the British horsemen rode across the battlefield, the exhausted French soldiers dropped their guns and ran for their lives. Arthur beamed happily. "By God," he shouted. "I never saw anything so beautiful in my life!"

The French fled and the British took control of Spain.

After the battle, Arthur met one of the greatest Spanish painters, Francisco José de Goya y Lucientes (usually just called "Goya"). Arthur posed for a portrait.

Every few minutes, another officer rushed up to his commander, delivering another piece of news about the army or bringing information about the French from a spy. Despite all these interruptions, Goya painted an extraordinary portrait. Today, you can see it hanging in the National Gallery in London.

From Salamanca, Arthur led his army to Madrid, the capital of Spain. They were greeted by rapturous crowds. People tried to cut off pieces of Arthur's clothing to keep for good luck. Women flocked around the British soldiers, kissing and hugging them. To the amazement of the British, the Spanish men tried to kiss them too. "What's going on?" said the British to one another. "Chaps shouldn't kiss other chaps."

Just like his men, Arthur was rather embarrassed. The Spanish never stopped shouting, waving their arms and kissing one another. Arthur preferred people who only spoke when they had something useful to say.

Worst of all, the Spaniards stank of garlic.

Throughout Madrid, the parties continued into the night, but Arthur went to bed early and he got up early the following morning. After breakfasting on a boiled egg and some buttered toast, he unrolled the map and plotted his next move.

Arthur's capture of Madrid was reported all over

Europe. It was a great triumph for the British and a bitter humiliation for the French. The British government promoted Arthur – he was now the Earl of Wellington – and gave him enough money to buy a big house in the English countryside.

The Spanish were equally grateful, and invited Arthur to take control of their army. He now had a huge force of men. Together, the British, Spanish and Portuguese armies totalled a hundred thousand men. Previously, he had been facing French armies ten times the size of his own. Now, the French had only twice as many men as him. At the same time, Arthur had the support of ordinary people in the Spanish and Portuguese countryside. Farmers, blacksmiths, teachers, priests, shopkeepers, bakers – all of them supported the British and hated the French.

Wherever Arthur led his army, he took great care that his men did not upset the locals, and he created a special force of military police to enforce discipline. If a soldier was found stealing a chicken or sneaking honey from a bee hive, he would be whipped. If a soldier attacked the local women or fought the local men, he would be hanged. Arthur forbade his men from stealing food or drink, even if they were starving. He understood a simple fact: when you are travelling through a foreign country, your travels will be much more difficult if the inhabitants hate you. Make friends with the locals, and they will help you with everything.

If you included this huge army of Spanish saboteurs and spies, all fighting for the British, you could say that Arthur had many more people fighting for him than Napoleon did. They waged "guerrilla war" – which means war waged by civilians rather than soldiers. The word "guerrilla" derives from the Spanish word for "war" – "guerra".

In the guerrilla war that consumed Spain, men and women fought side by side. Priests and farmers, bakers and housewives – the Spanish people joined together and fought against the French invaders.

If Napoleon had been able to come to Spain himself, perhaps he would have swept these ramshackle armies aside. His tactical genius would have destroyed any Spanish resistance. However, he was too busy fighting on the other side of Europe. With a huge army, he had invaded Russia and marched on Moscow. He couldn't spare any time or energy for Spain. So he had sent his second-best generals instead. It was a terrible mistake.

***

As autumn descended into winter, and the rains fell, Arthur withdrew back to Portugal. The winter was spent training and equipping his men. Every day, they cleaned their rifles and polished their boots. Arthur pored over maps and discussed tactics with his officers. Day by day, week by week, Arthur turned his army into a perfect fighting machine.

One of the factors that made Arthur such a great general was his concern for the welfare of his soldiers. Once, for instance, he rode thirty miles to visit some wounded soldiers. He discovered that they were lying in draughty shelters made from leaves and branches, while their officers slept in comfortable lodgings with windows and roofs. So Arthur ordered a swap. He told the officers to make way for the wounded. Then he rode away. The next day, he came back to check that his orders had been implemented. They had not. The officers had ignored him, and were still sleeping in the comfortable beds, leaving their wounded men outside. Arthur was so furious that he threw the officers out of their beds and sacked them from their jobs. The wounded men were carried inside and laid down in comfort.

Such behaviour made ordinary British soldiers love their general. He would force them to work immensely hard, and go without sleep for days, and march for many miles, and fight until they had no energy left in their bodies, but he would also take care of them. In return, they fought for him with exceptional skill and bravery.

When the fighting stopped, they did not behave so well. Every battle ended with a few days of craziness. Arthur's soldiers loved drinking. After one battle, Arthur toured the town, and found several of his men in a cellar, surrounded by broken barrels and open bottles, literally swimming in wine.

In those crazy days after the end of a battle, Arthur couldn't do much to stop his men from stealing. At other times, he was extremely fierce with them. Any soldier found stealing from the local population would be flogged. "If you want something," said Arthur, "then you must pay for it."

In the spring of 1813, Arthur marched his men towards the French. As he crossed the border between Portugal and Spain, he wheeled his horse around on the spot. "Farewell, Portugal!" shouted Arthur, waving his hat in the air. "I shall never see you again."

And he never did.

Arthur drove the French to the north of Spain. The French retreated into the seaside town of San Sebastian, and Arthur surrounded them. Day after day, British and French guns fired at one another. Day after day, the French grew hungrier and thirstier. Day after day, the stench was more disgusting. It was August. The sun was so hot that people could barely move. After seventy-three days, and a terrifying thunderstorm, the British finally broke through the French defences. They swept through the town, killing everyone that they found, setting fire to all the houses. By the end of that long, brutal night, every street in San Sebastian except one had been burnt to the ground.

Today, San Sebastian is a smart town with a beautiful beach, but the inhabitants have not forgotten the seige. Every year, a procession marches through the one street that survived the fire, carrying candles, remembering the horror of that day in 1813.

Arthur urged his army onwards. He forced the French back into France and, for the first time, made his camp on French soil. Here, Arthur had a lucky escape. He was riding with a Spanish officer who suddenly shouted out, "Ah! I have been hit!"

"Where?" said Arthur.

"In my bottom," said the Spaniard. A bullet had punctured his bum.

Arthur couldn't help laughing.

At that very moment, a second bullet smacked into Arthur's leg, hitting his sword and cutting his thigh. He stopped laughing and started cursing. The wound wasn't too serious, but he had to stop riding for a week, which he found very frustrating.

Arthur marched his men further into France. They headed for Toulouse. A few hours after they occupied the city, a messenger arrived from Paris. Peace had been declared. Napoleon had abdicated.

For once, Arthur could not resist showing his emotions. He jumped up, and started dancing on the spot, clicking his fingers and singing – just like a Spaniard.

CHAPTER SEVEN

On May 3, Arthur received the news that he had been made a duke. He was now Arthur Wellesley, the Duke of Wellington. The following day, he arrived in Paris and took up his new post as the British Ambassador to France.

On the same day, Napoleon was exiled from Italy to his new home – Elba.

The journey didn't take long: Elba is a small island about five miles from Italy, just off the coast of Tuscany. Arriving in his new home, Napoleon was treated extremely well. He was allowed a thousand men as his own personal escort, and given an honorary title: the Emperor of Elba.

Other men might have settled down to a comfortable retirement, or started writing their memoirs. Not

Napoleon. Disliking the government of Elba, he rewrote the laws and imposed a new set of rules on the population. When that got boring, he turned his attention to a more dangerous pursuit: plotting his return to France.

With Napoleon gone, Arthur worked in Paris, helping to decide how Europe and France would be ruled. New borders were drawn. New governments were created. New laws were written.

After a month in Paris, Arthur finally rode in a carriage to the coast and took a ship to England. At Dover, a huge crowd awaited him. All the way to London, they lined the road, cheering and shouting. In London, a group of men waited for his carriage. They wanted to remove the horses, grab Arthur and carry him on their shoulders. Arthur stepped aside, jumped onto his horse and galloped through the streets alone.

Outside his own house, he dismounted, and handed the horse to a servant. "Welcome home, sir," said the man.

Arthur thanked him, and hurried into the house. There, he found his wife and children. He had been gone for five years. His two sons had been babies when he last saw them. Now they were boys aged seven and six. "Hello," said Arthur in a calm voice, smiling at them as if he had just been gone for a couple of hours.

The two boys stared at him. They did not recognise this tall man. They could not remember ever seeing him before.

"That's your father," said Kitty. "Go and say hello to him."

Slowly, nervously, the two boys walked across the room to their father. He leaned down, and shook hands with each of them.

With the public, Arthur was equally formal. He may have been the greatest hero in the country, but he stayed the same man: quiet, humble, stern, silent and calm. When people lined the streets to cheer him, he just nodded and smiled. When huge parties were thrown in his honour, he ate little, drank less and hardly spoke at all. But he was always accompanied by his officers, and they made up for him – they ate hugely, and drank deeply, and shouted loudly, and danced all night.

Arthur was forty-five years old. He was famous and rich. He had a wife and two sons. He could do whatever he wanted with his life.

Now, he just had to decide what he wanted to do.

The government soon asked Arthur to continue working as a diplomat, and so he went to France. At parties in Paris, he had the strange experience of meeting the generals whom he had been fighting for the past few years. Although he had never met any of them before, he knew exactly what they looked like, because he had spent every day staring at them through his telescope. When he met Marshal Massena, who had been such a difficult opponent in Spain, they had a very friendly chat. Massena said, "You know what? You should buy me dinner."

"Why?"

"Because you made me starve so many times."

"No, *you* should buy me dinner," said Arthur. "Because you stopped me sleeping so many times."

From Paris, Arthur visited Brussels, then moved to Vienna, where he continued working as a diplomat. He negotiated with ambassadors from other countries, and they discussed the future of Europe.

And then, before Arthur could think any more about what to do with the rest of his life, the decision was made for him. At the beginning of March 1815, some startling news came from France.

A few days earlier, on February 26th, Napoleon had boarded a boat in Elba. Accompanied by a thousand soldiers and six boats, he had sailed across the Mediterranean and landed on the south coast of France.

The prisoner had escaped. The Emperor wanted his crown back.

Napoleon rode through the countryside, gathering troops and support. Wherever he went, he was greeted by cheering crowds. Across France, men were hurrying to join his army.

Who could stop him?

CHAPTER EIGHT

The Tsar of Russia walked through the crowded room, and reached Arthur. Stretching out his arm, the Tsar laid his hand on Arthur's shoulder and said, "It is for you to save the world again."

All the countries of Europe depended on the Duke of Wellington. They trusted him to work the same magic that he had performed in Portugal and Spain. They believed that he, and only he, could defeat the great French army and its magnificent general, Napoleon Bonaparte.

If Arthur was flattered, nervous or excited, he did not show it. He simply smiled and nodded, and promised to do his best.

Arthur left Vienna and headed for Brussels, arriving on the 4 April, where he was appointed to command the British army.

There were spies everywhere. Many Belgians had served in Napoleon's armies. The French had occupied Belgium from 1794 to 1814. No one knew who favoured the British and who favoured the French. Anyone might be a friend or an enemy. The postal service still carried letters between Brussels and Paris. Every day, people sent news back and forth. It was impossible to keep secrets. Rumours rushed around the cities and countryside. "Napoleon is marching towards us now," whispered someone.

"He has boarded a boat and sailed to America," said another.

"The British have retreated to Antwerp," said a third.

"The British are marching on Paris," said a fourth.

Everyone knew everything. No one knew anything.

But Arthur knew that there was only one way to make sure that the French did not discover his plans: tell no one what his plans were. He gathered information from everywhere, but discussed his plans with only his closest friends and most loyal officers.

For several weeks, Arthur and Napoleon stayed in their respective cities – Brussels and Paris – gathering their armies and planning what to do next.

Each waited for the other to make the first move. But nothing happened.

Finally, Napoleon left Paris on 12 June. Summer had arrived. The weather was perfect for fighting. He had gathered an army of a hundred and twenty thousand men. They marched north towards Brussels. If Napoleon defeated the British army, he could rule Europe. If he lost... well, Napoleon never even considered the possibility that he might lose. He knew that he was the greatest military commander in Europe, and no one was good enough to beat him.

If anyone had been watching Arthur, they would have seen a man who seemed to be completely calm and happy. He watched cricket matches. He went to smart dinners. He seemed to do nothing except enjoy himself. When the Duchess of Richmond asked if she should cancel the large, extravagant party that she was planning, he told her not to be ridiculous. "Duchess, you may give your ball with the greatest safety," said Arthur. So she continued buying candles and bottles of wine, preparing for the biggest party that Brussels had seen for years.

***

It was the day of the Duchess of Richmond's ball. In the morning, news arrived that Napoleon had crossed the border between France and Belgium. He was on his way! And Arthur still did nothing. People began to get restless and nervous. Was he never going to summon his troops? Would he just continue watching cricket matches and going to parties – even when Napoleon marched up to the gates of Brussels?

Arthur's calm had a simple explanation. He knew that Napoleon's spies were watching everything that he did. So, he was very careful never to show his feelings. If any spies were watching, they would have seen a man who seemed entirely uninterested in war.

That night, hundreds of glamorous and beautiful people assembled at the ballroom hired by the Duchess of Richmond. A band played. Waiters weaved through the crowd carrying trays. Officers in glittering uniforms danced with women in long flowing dresses.

Towards midnight, a startling piece of news arrived: the French were only twenty miles from Brussels. French troops had attacked the Prussians, who had been forced to retreat. The battle had begun. But when he was told this terrifying news, Arthur merely smiled and said, "Let the party continue."

When people asked if he wasn't going to join his

soldiers and fight the French, he shook his head. "No, no. Let's enjoy ourselves. I'll take care of Napoleon when I'm ready."

Everyone was very impressed by his calm. If any French spies lurked among the partygoers, they would tell their bosses that the Duke of Wellington appeared immensely confident of victory. And if any of the British, Prussians or Belgians were feeling a little nervous, then Arthur's cool nerves calmed them down.

Arthur danced with a few of the ladies, and sipped a little wine, then wandered across the room and whispered to his host, the Duke of Richmond, "I say, sir, do you have a map in the house?"

"Of course."

"Could I see it?"

"Follow me."

They walked slowly through the ballroom, stopping every few paces to chat with one of the other partygoers, then reached a door and slipped into the dark library. The Duke of Richmond closed the door behind them. Immediately, Arthur changed. His smile vanished. His voice was brisk and business-like. "Where's the map, then? Over here?" He hurried to the table, and unrolled a large map of the surrounding countryside. Staring at the roads and villages, drawn in brown ink on the crinkly paper, Arthur shook his head. "He's got twenty-four hours on me."

His host stared at him, blinking. "What are you going to do?"

"Fight him here," said Arthur, and placed his finger on a small village called Waterloo.

They shook hands, and Arthur sneaked out of the house, leaving by a door that could not be seen by all the guests. He didn't want anyone at the party to know that he was concerned by the news of Napoleon's march.

That night, Arthur got only two hours sleep. Early in the morning, he rushed south, leading his army towards the French. Brussels was a scene of frantic activity. Men ran through the streets. Everywhere, you could hear the sound of trumpets and drumming. Many officers had not even managed to change out of the smart clothes that they were wearing at the Duchess of Richmond's party, and joined their regiments in dancing-shoes.

Arthur went first to the crossroads at Quatre Bras, where the British army was waiting, then to Brie, above the village of Ligny, where Field Marshal Blücher had drawn up the Prussians. They discussed tactics, then Arthur was called back to the British lines. The French had attacked. As Arthur rode away and headed for his troops, he saw more French soldiers marching towards the Prussian positions. Smoke gushed into the sky. The sound of cannons echoed across the landscape. The battle had begun.

By the time that Arthur reached his troops, the battle was almost over. The French had reached Quatre Bras.

If the French had surged forwards at that moment, they would probably have beaten the British. But Marshal Ney did not advance his troops until the middle of the afternoon. By then, Arthur had ridden back to take personal command of the British troops.

His presence, and the reinforcements that he summoned, stiffened the British lines. The French were beaten back.

Meanwhile, Blücher and the Prussian army had lost ground to the French. Sixteen thousand Prussians were killed. Blücher himself had been thrown to the ground when his horse was shot, and would have been taken prisoner if one of his men hadn't thrown a cloak over him, hiding all the medals pinned to his chest. The Prussians turned and fled.

When Arthur learnt of Blücher's disastrous retreat, he realised that he must retreat too. In the pouring rain, the British turned their backs on the French and marched towards Brussels. They stopped on a ridge beside the small village of Waterloo. At their backs, a thick forest prevented anyone creeping up behind them. They camped there.

The French may have thought that they had beaten both the British and the Prussians, but they had actually done exactly what Arthur wanted: he had now chosen the exact spot where the battle would be fought. If Napoleon was going to defeat the British, he would have to send his soldiers across the fields and up the ridge. If the British fought them off, and held on to the ridge, they would win the battle. It was the type of battle that Arthur knew best: his men would withstand attack after attack, and then, when the enemy finally ran out of energy, charge down on them.

Throughout that long night, the rain fell. The men lay on the ground. They were wet, cold and hungry. Each man knew that he might die in the morning.

The British second-in-command, Lord Uxbridge, went to see Arthur and asked about his plans for the next day. But he didn't have much success. As always, Arthur refused to give much away. When Uxbridge complained about the lack of information, Arthur said, "Who will attack first in the morning? Napoleon or me?"

"Napoleon," replied Lord Uxbridge.

"Well, Napoleon has not told me where he will attack," said Arthur. "And he has not told me when he will attack. My plans depend entirely on what he does. So, how do you expect me to tell you my plans?"

Lord Uxbridge had no answer to that.

Arthur smiled. "There is one thing for certain," he said. "Whatever happens, you and I will do our duty."

And that was all he would say about his plans for the following day.

You might have thought that the second-in-command would get told the battle plans. After all, if

Arthur had been killed or wounded, Lord Uxbridge would have taken over as commander of the troops. But Arthur refused to tell him anything.

That night, Arthur went to bed at midnight. He rose again at three o'clock. Once more, he consulted the map, discussed tactics with his officers and inspected his men.

By dawn on Sunday the 18 June 1815, the rain had dwindled to a light drizzle. Across the murky fields, the armies faced one another.

For the British soldiers, breakfast was a few biscuits and a sip of rum. They cleaned their daggers and their guns. They wrote letters to their wives and families. And then they waited.

Arthur stood on the ridge. He put his telescope to his eye, and stared at the landscape. He lowered the telescope, looked at his officers and nodded. Although he said nothing, they knew exactly what he meant. He was ready.

CHAPTER NINE

On the opposite side of the battlefield, Napoleon was feeling confident. He surveyed the ground, and felt sure that he was staring at the sight of a famous victory. When one of his generals warned him that Wellington was a clever commander, Napoleon laughed.

"Just because you have been beaten by Wellington, you think he is a great general," said Napoleon. "But you're wrong. Wellington is a bad general. The English are bad troops. This battle will be a picnic."

When another officer tried to argue with him, Napoleon shook his head and walked away, throwing one final remark over his shoulder: "*Nous coucherons ce soir a Bruxelles,*" he said. Which means: "Tonight, we shall sleep in Brussels."

The officers looked at one another. They were worried. One of them said, "What shall we do?"

Another asked, "Who is the greatest general on the planet?"

"Napoleon," replied the first officer.

"Exactly. So trust him. If he believes that we will win today, then we will win. Now, don't you have work to do?"

The officers hurried in different directions, heading towards their men. As they left, each of them said "goodbye" and "good luck" to the others. None of them knew if they would still be alive by the end of the day.

Napoleon had a very simple plan. He intended to march directly at the British, smash a hole through the middle of their lines, and divide the army in half. They would be disorientated, disorganized and cut off from their commanders. It would be easy – Napoleon was sure of that.

For years, Napoleon had been winning battles all over Europe with cunning and brilliance. For some strange reason, he planned to win at Waterloo with nothing except brute force. Perhaps all the spaghetti that he had eaten on Elba had addled his brain. It had certainly added to his stomach. When Napoleon won his most famous victories, he had been slim and fit.

Now, he was plump and easily tired. Every few minutes, he had to get down from his horse and sit in a nice comfy chair until he felt more energetic.

Although Napoleon's plan was simple and obvious, it might have worked. If Napoleon had allowed his gunners to spend longer bombing the British lines, for instance, perhaps he would have been more successful. But he let them fire for only half an hour, then halted the guns and gave the order for his infantry and cavalry to move forward.

The weather also made a huge difference to the battle.

After so much rain, the earth was squidgy.

Imagine what happens when you fire a cannonball. If the ground is hard and dry, the cannonball will bounce. It will hit a soldier, and bounce, and hit another soldier, and bounce again, perhaps smashing into ten or twenty men before finally rolling to a halt. When the ground is soft and soggy, a cannonball will hit a man, then stop. Rather than killing twenty men, each cannonball will only kill one.

The French troops started marching towards the British. With every footstep that they took, their boots sank into the mud.

Up on the ridge, Arthur had ordered his men to lie

down and wait. "Be patient," he ordered them. "Wait for the Frenchies to come here. Then we'll have them."

The British soldiers lay down in the mud. They were cold. Their clothes were soaked with water. Their teeth chattered. They could hear the roar of cannonballs, the shriek of bullets and the screams of wounded men. They lay still. Some of them closed their eyes. One or two even fell asleep. The others just waited for the order to get up.

Behind them, Arthur waited too. He peered through his telescope, waiting for the first sight of the enemy.

The French marched through the fields and up to the ridge. They were confused. They couldn't see any English troops. And then, just when they reached the top of the ridge, they heard an English voice shouting.

"Up and at 'em! Fire, boys! Fire!"

On the top of the ridge, the English troops leaped to their feet, put their muskets to their shoulders and fired. A hail of bullets rained down on the French.

The battle continued for hours. Arthur had almost seventy thousand men. Opposite him, Napoleon had about five thousand more. But Blücher was marching towards them, bringing with him the Prussian army.

Blücher had been wounded on the previous afternoon, but he was now propped on his horse, eating rhubarb and drinking schnapps. (Apparently, rhubarb and schnapps is the perfect cure for wounds. That's what Blücher thought, anyway.) If Blücher arrived in time, he would sweep into the side of the French army and knock them to pieces. But if Blücher was late, the French would have time to destroy the British, then turn around and destroy the Prussians too.

Throughout the afternoon, swarms of French soldiers marched towards the ridge. The British stood their ground, and refused to be moved.

Wave after wave of French soldiers thudded against the British lines, and wave after wave was beaten back.

In the middle of the afternoon, Blücher finally arrived at the battlefield with the Prussian army. They charged from the east, and attacked the unprotected French flank.

Suddenly, Napoleon had to fight in two different places at the same time.

If Napoleon had been a different type of man, he would have chosen this moment to retreat. It was late in the afternoon. His men had been fighting all day. They were wet, tired and hungry. Napoleon could have drawn back, taken up a defensive position, and spent the night considering what to do next. But he wasn't a cautious man. He was a gambler. He took big risks. So he sent an order to Marshall Ney. "Charge!"

Ney led the French cavalry across the battlefield and charged directly at the British lines.

Line after line of horses charged at the British soldiers. Time after time, they were beaten back.

The British had a simple system. The infantry stood in two rows. The first row fired their muskets while the men in the second row knelt and reloaded. Then the first row kneeled down to reload, and the second row stood up to fire. And then they swapped over again. They fired and reloaded, fired and reloaded, fired and reloaded, destroying anyone or anything that came close.

The smoke was suffocating. The sound was terrible.

Everyone was deafened by the groans of wounded men and the screams of horses and the roar of guns and the shouting of officers desperately trying to control their men. Blood soaked into the wet ground. Wherever you looked, you would see a heap of dead and dying men. The earth was littered with torn clothes and discarded hats and smashed swords and dropped guns and feet and arms and legs and heads and hands which had been detached from their bodies.

At seven o'clock, at the end of a long and bloody day, Napoleon threw his final weapon into the battle.

The Imperial Guard were the best troops on the planet. They had never lost a battle. To reward their brilliance, they were paid twice as much as other troops in the French army, and fed on double rations. Fearless and reckless, they inspired terror wherever they fought.

All day, the Imperial Guard had been saving their energy. All day, they had been lying on their knapsacks, smoking their pipes, waiting for the order to attack. Now it came.

Napoleon gave the order. The Imperial Guard charged.

"Vive l'Empereur!" they shouted. *"Vive l'Empereur!"* They swept across the battlefield, and headed for the British lines.

They marched across the battlefield, treading on the dead and the wounded.

The drums beat in time to their footsteps.

They marched up to the ridge.

They could see nothing ahead of them. No soldiers. No guns. Nothing. So they just kept marching.

And then they heard an English voice. A voice that shouted: "Stand up, Guards!"

A line of British soldiers leaped up from the grass. They had been lying down in the mud, hiding. Now, they raised their rifles.

The English voice shouted once more: "Fire!"

A thousand British rifles fired. A thousand British bullets crashed into the French lines. And before the French could even take a breath, the British fired again. And fired again. And then they fired once more.

Over the noise of screams and gunpowder, they could hear an English voice. The voice of their general. He shouted as loudly as he could: "Now's your time, my boys! Charge! Charge!"

A mass of British men charged down the hillside, their sharpened bayonets glittering in the late afternoon sunlight.

The Imperial Guard may have been the best troops on the planet. They may never have lost a battle. They may have been waiting all day for the chance to do some proper fighting. But when they saw the British army racing towards them, they didn't even hesitate. They turned and fled.

Arthur saw that the moment had arrived to take control of the battle. The French were wavering. With one great punch, he could knock them out. He closed his telescope and rode to the edge of the ridge. Waving his hat, he shouted at his men: "Go forward, boys, and secure your victory!"

The British cavalry plunged down the hill and roared towards the French lines.

The French ran for their lives.

Following his troops, Arthur rode across the battlefield with Lord Uxbridge. A French cannonball whistled through the air and crashed into Lord Uxbridge's knee. He looked down. "By God," said Lord Uxbridge. "I've lost my leg."

Arthur turned to have a look. "By God, sir, so you have."

They both nodded, and stared at the remains of Lord Uxbridge's leg, which had been smashed to pieces by the cannonball. The stump was dripping blood.

Some soldiers ran forward to help Lord Uxbridge from his horse, and when Arthur was certain that his second-in-command was in safe hands, he galloped onwards to continue surveying the battle.

Lord Uxbridge was carried to a tent, where doctors chopped off the rest of his leg and cleaned the wound. During the operation, Lord Uxbridge never screamed. He never even moaned. He only spoke once during the entire operation: he gestured at the surgeon's knife, and said, "I say, sir! Your knife is a little blunt! Next time, would you mind sharpening it first?"

Back on the battlefield, the British charged down from the ridge, sweeping the enemy before them. The Prussians pressed forward from the east. Caught between two rampaging armies, the French retreated.

Arthur rode at the front of his troops. When his troops saw him, they cheered and waved their rifles. In reply, he lifted his hat.

One of Arthur's officers tried to persuade him that he should stay at the back, protected from the final barrages of French bullets and cannonballs.

"Never mind," said Arthur. "Let them fire away."

The officer insisted, "Your life is too valuable to throw away."

"The battle is won," replied Arthur. "My life is of no consequence now."

CHAPTER TEN

As the sun sank in the sky, the battle ended. The French army collapsed. Napoleon jumped onto a horse and rode towards Paris, leaving his luggage and his men on the battlefield.

At nine o'clock that night, Arthur met Marshal Blücher. The two commanders shook hands. They spoke to one another in French, since Blücher knew no English and Arthur knew no German. They congratulated one another on a famous victory.

Very slowly, Arthur rode the five miles back to his lodgings. He stopped every few paces to exchange some words with his exhausted soldiers. The ground was littered with hats, guns, feathers, helmets, swords and bodies. Wounded men groaned and begged for help. Robbers sneaked from corpse to corpse, stealing valuables.

Reaching the inn where his bed had been made, Arthur ordered his cook to bring dinner. With a few of his officers who had not been wounded, Arthur sat down to eat. They didn't talk much. At the end of the meal, Arthur walked to his bedroom, lay down without washing or undressing, and fell asleep immediately.

He was woken by a doctor bringing a list of casualties. The doctor read out every name on the list, and Arthur wept. Tears trickled down his blackened face, which was still covered with mud and soot. He hadn't had time to wash.

Tens of thousands of men had died. The morning after the battle, the fields were still awash with blood. Wounded men lay in the grass, moaning and groaning, begging for help. But there weren't enough doctors. Many of the men lay there until they died.

Arthur had won the greatest battle of his life, but he wasn't triumphant. He didn't dance or sing. He hardly even smiled. He knew how many men had lost their lives. He understood the true horror of war.

Several years later, Arthur was talking to a woman who wanted to know all about the battles that he had fought. She said, "What a glorious thing must be a victory, sir."

Arthur shook his head and replied, "The greatest tragedy in the world, Madam, except a defeat."

CHAPTER ELEVEN

After the battle of Waterloo, Arthur stayed in France for three years, working as a diplomat. Several supporters of Napoleon tried to kill him. They wanted to take revenge for their hero's defeat. But the bullets always missed Arthur. Just like on the battlefield, he was impossible to kill.

In 1817, he bought two homes. In London, he bought Apsley House, which had previously belonged to his brother. In Hampshire, he bought a mansion in the countryside called Stratfield Saye. The following year, he moved back to England, started living in his two houses, and hardly ever left Britain again. Having spent most of his life travelling around the world, he now wanted to settle down in his own country.

Not long after Arthur's return to London, he lost

two of the most important people in his life.

After Waterloo, Napoleon Bonaparte had been banished to St Helena – a small island in the middle of the Atlantic Ocean. The same small island that Arthur had visited on his way back from India. After six unhappy years there, Napoleon died.

Throughout Europe, people felt a great sense of relief. They could finally stop worrying that Napoleon would somehow find a way to escape from St Helena, get to France and make another attempt to win back his empire.

A few years later, Arthur's wife Kitty died, too. Their marriage had always been unhappy. With his soldiers, Arthur had been generous and patient. He had coaxed nervous young men to become brave warriors, and inspired thousands of troops with his own courage and good humour. But with his wife, he had been different. He had always been grumpy towards her, always rude, always aggressive. And when she died, he didn't seem to miss her much.

Napoleon had gone. Kitty had gone. There were no more battles to fight. Arthur was the greatest soldier in Europe, but peace had been declared. What could he do now? Should he put his feet up and enjoy life? Should he devote his days to eating and drinking and reading and chatting and having a good time? Should he spend the rest of his days in a comfy armchair?

Of course not. Arthur was happiest when he was working. He stopped being a soldier, and became a politician instead. He took his seat in the House of Commons. He joined the government.

Like most people, Arthur became more conservative as he got older. He was a snob. He despised democracy. According to him, the common people didn't know what was good for them. They should shut up and do what they were told. These views made him very popular with the King and the aristocracy, but very unpopular with ordinary people. He survived several assassination attempts. A crowd attacked his house, and smashed the windows with stones. They only ran away when one of Arthur's servants emerged from the house with a gun and shot at them.

Politics was a lot more exciting in those days. After a fierce disagreement with one of his harshest critics, Lord Winchilsea, Arthur challenged him to a duel. Lord Winchilsea accepted. They met at Battersea. Each of them had a pistol. They took a few paces apart and waited for the signal to shoot.

"Fire!"

At the last moment, the two old men realised that

killing one another was a little bit pointless. Lord Winchilsea fired into the ground, and Arthur fired into the air.

Shooting people isn't the best way to run a country, but it was the way that Arthur knew best. He found ordinary politics extremely frustrating. He may have been a successful leader in wartime, but he was less successful in peacetime. He lacked the skills of a good politician, and preferred soldiers to civilians. Arthur was invited to become Prime Minister in 1828. He served for two years, but resigned in November 1830.

However, even after leaving the cabinet, Arthur could still offer the benefits of his common sense and honesty. When Queen Victoria came to the throne, he was one of her most frequent advisers.

In his last years, Arthur held a number of important posts. He was commander-in-chief of the army, Chancellor of Oxford University, lord lieutenant of Hampshire and constable of the Tower of London. He was also appointed Lord Warden of the Cinque Ports, a job that came with a house, Walmer Castle, in Kent. When he visited, he would always sleep on an army camp bed, just as if he was still camping beside a battlefield in Portugal or Spain.

He devoted much of his time to riding and hunting.

Every day, he received letters, not just from friends or colleagues, but ordinary people who sought his advice or offered their own to him. Arthur had several secretaries to answer these letters, but he almost always added a few words of his own. As with everything else in his life, his letters were quick, efficient and brutally honest.

CHAPTER TWELVE

On 14 September 1852, Arthur sat in his favourite yellow armchair in Walmer Castle. He took a few sips of tea, then closed his eyes. A minute or two later, he was dead.

He was eighty-three years old.

His funeral was one of the biggest ever seen in Britain. Millions of people lined the streets. Twelve horses pulled the funeral carriage through London, and delivered Arthur to St Paul's Cathedral, where he was buried.

Today, Wellington is remembered in many different ways. A boot bears his name. So does the capital of New Zealand. And fifty-seven streets in London.

But Arthur Wellesley, the Duke of Wellington, will always be remembered most for what happened on

18 June 1815 – that rainy day when he faced his greatest opponent across the muddy fields of Waterloo.

TIMELINE

1769	Arthur is born on May 1 in Dublin
1781	He is sent to Eton College
1785	Living in Brussels with his mother
1786	Training at the Academy of Equitation at Angers
1787	Joins army
1788	Arrives in Ireland
1796	Sails to India
1799	Battle of Seringapatam and death of Tipu Sultan
1803	Battle of Assaye
1805	Leaves India and returns to London
1806	Serves as Member of Parliament for Rye in Sussex
1806	Marries Kitty Pakenham on April 10
1807	First child born on Feb 3: Arthur Richard Wellesley. A year later, Kitty has another son, Charles
1809	Sails to Portugal as commander of the British force
1812	Battle of Salamanca and entry of the British Army into Madrid
1814	Receives his title on May 3; he is now Arthur Wellesley, the Duke of Wellington. Napoleon sails to Elba on May 4

1815	Napoleon escapes from Elba on February 26. On June 18, Napoleon and Wellington fight the battle of Waterloo.
1820	Wellington is appointed Lord-Lieutenant of Hampshire
1828	Serves as Prime Minister until 1830
1831	Wellington's wife dies on April 24
1852	Arthur dies on September 14 at Walmer Castle. Buried in St Pauls on November 18

QUIZ

After you've finished the book, test yourself and see how well you remember what you've read.

1. What did the Wellesley family never manage to agree on?
    Who should sit in the front passenger seat
    The best way to spell their name
    How long it took to boil an egg

2. Arthur's mother took him away from Eton College because:
    He was in love with the headteacher's daughter
    She didn't like the school uniform
    He wasn't learning anything

3. When Kitty rejected Arthur's proposal of marriage, he:
    Wrote her a love song that became a No. 1 hit in Ireland
    Threw his violin on to a bonfire in the woods outside Dublin
    Decided he fancied her best friend more anyway

4. What did Arthur take with him on his voyage to India?
    500 books
    250 preserved quail eggs
    100 drawings of Kitty

5. Why was Tipu Sultan, the ruler of Mysore, known as 'The Tiger'?
    Because he dyed his beard in yellow and black stripes
    Because he had a reputation for being ferocious
    Because he purred when his tummy was stroked

6. What was the recommended treatment for the itchy rash that

Arthur caught while in India?
   Bathing in acid
   Eating a ripe mango every hour on the hour
   Applying an ointment invented by Henry VIII

7. Arthur was able to communicate with the people of Seringapatam by:
   Talking very slowly and loudly in English
   Speaking the local dialect fluently in a strong Irish accent
   Using an interpreter but checking the translation against his knowledge of a few basic words

8. Arthur led his troops to victory at the Battle of Assaye bespite being outnumbered:
   2:1
   5:1
   7:1

9. While Arthur was in India, Britain formed an alliance against Napoleon with:
   Australia and Tibet
   Austria and Russia
   Albania and Norway

10. When Arthur saw Kitty again for the first time in ten years, he said:
   'By Jove, she has grown ugly!'
   'Omigod, what a minger!'
   'I do believe she will make an excellent candidate for a reality TV make-over show!'

11. Why were the Spanish furious with Napoleon?
   Because he had kidnapped Real Madrid's star striker

Because he made his brother King of Spain
Because he banned bull-fighting on the grounds of animal cruelty

12. What did the commander of the French army do after blowing up the bridges across the River Douro?
    Ordered his lunch for the next day and went to bed
    Lined the banks with cannons ready to fire
    Went for a swim to show that he was not afraid

13. What was the name of the fortifications built to protect Lisbon?
    The lines of Torres Vedras
    The Jose Mourinho defences
    The ditches of Torremolinos

14. What did British soldiers find strange about the way the Spanish people celebrated after the French were driven out of Spain?
    Women performed cartwheels
    Men kissed men
    Children dressed up as animals

15. What did Arthur do when a Spanish officer was shot in the bum?
    Offered to take him to hospital by piggyback
    Shot him in the foot as well to take his mind off it
    Laughed out loud

16. Why was Arthur's career as a diplomat brought to a sudden end in 1815?
    His wife Kitty gave birth to triplets and insisted that he helped look after the babies

Napoleon escaped from Elba and started a revolt in France
He was forced to resign after falling asleep during a state banquet in honour of the Russian Tsar

17. What did Arthur tell people to do when he heard that French troops were outside Brussels?
　　Carry on partying
　　Run for their lives
　　Man the barricades

18. What did British soldiers have for breakfast before the Battle of Waterloo?
　　Sausage, egg and chips and a cup of tea
　　A packet of crisps and a bottle of Lucozade
　　A few dry biscuits and a swig of rum

19. What did Napoleon's Imperial Guard do during most of the battle?
　　Make daring charges against the British cannons
　　Lounge around smoking their pipes
　　Polish the buttons on their uniforms to make sure they looked their best

20. In which of his homes did the Duke of Wellington die?
　　Walmer Castle in Kent
　　Apsley House in London
　　Stratfield Saye in Hampshire

Dear reader,

Thousands of books have been written about the Duke of Wellington, and thousands more about the battle of Waterloo. These three are particularly interesting and useful:

Wellington: a personal history by Christopher Hibbert

Wellington by Richard Holmes

Wellington by Elizabeth Longford. (This biography is divided into two volumes: *The Years of the Sword* stops at the battle of Waterloo and *Pillar of State* describes the rest of Arthur's life.)

You can visit three of the Duke of Wellington's houses: Apsley House in London, Stratfield Saye in Hampshire and Walmer Castle in Kent. If you go to Walmer Castle, you can see the yellow armchair in which he died.

Also in London, you can visit a huge model of the battle of Waterloo, built by William Siborne, and now displayed at the National Army Museum in Chelsea. The story behind the model is told in *Wellington's Smallest Victory* by Peter Hofschröer. In the National Gallery, you can see Goya's portrait of Wellington.

In India, Spain, Portugal and Belgium, you can visit the places where Wellington fought his greatest battles. Some of the battlefields have hardly changed since Arthur was there. Salamanca in Spain, for instance, looks almost exactly as it would have done when the British defeated the French there. In Belgium, the village of Waterloo has grown since 1815, but the fields and woodlands haven't changed much. You can stand just where Arthur stood with his telescope, surrounded by officers, peering through the smoke, watching the troops on the battlefield.

Wellington and the battle of Waterloo have featured in many

novels. Among the best are *Vanity Fair* by William Makepeace Thackeray and the *Sharpe* books by Bernard Cornwell, which follow a soldier in Wellington's army from 1799 to 1815.

Joshua Doder

Other titles in the WHO WAS... series:

WILLIAM SHAKESPEARE
The Mystery of the World's Greatest Playwright
Rupert Christiansen

Everyone has heard of plays like *Macbeth* and *A Midsummer Night's Dream*. But why do we know so little about the man who wrote them? Who exactly was William Shakespeare from Stratford-upon-Avon, and why do so many people believe that he was not the person he seemed to be?

This book is an exciting detective story, which goes back over four hundred years to the dramatic events of the reign of Queen Elizabeth I and explores the way that a brilliant and ambitious young man was caught up in a violent world of murder, revenge and treason.

ISBN: 1-904095-34-8

QUEEN VICTORIA
The Woman who Ruled the World
Kate Hubbard

Victoria was just 18 when she was crowned Queen in 1837 – a tiny figure with a will of iron. Never was there so queenly a queen. She made Britain great, and the people loved her for it.

In 1861 tragedy struck, when her husband Albert died. The little Queen loved dogs and cream cakes and the troops who fought her wars, but most of all she loved Albert. Dumb with grief, she hid herself away. Suddenly it seemed the woman who had made the monarchy so strong would destroy it. Could anyone persuade Victoria to be Queen again?

ISBN: 1-904095-32-1

MOZART
Child Genius
Gill Hornby

By the time he was four years old, it was clear that Wolfgang Amadeus Mozart was a musical genius. He could already play the clavier, the organ and the violin to perfection. When he was just seven, little Mozart began touring Europe, performing at court to Kings and Queens, and in concert halls to crowds of the paying public.

His father could see that his little Wolfgang would one day change the face of European music, and presumed that the adult Mozart would be wealthy, famous, adored around the world. What he did not know was how hard it can be for a child genius to grow up...

ISBN: 1-904977-64-2

BOUDICCA
Warrior Queen
Siân Busby

As Queen of Icenia in 1st Century AD Britain, married to her beloved Prasutagus, Boudicca lived a wonderful life. But then, after her husband weakened and died, and, with the ever-expanding Roman Empire making ever more impossible demands on her, young Boudicca was forced to stand up and defend her people.

Fearless and unprepared to compromise, Boudicca saw nothing to stop her going to war on her own. For her, slavery to Rome was not an option, even if this meant bloodshed and almost inevitable death...

ISBN: 1-904977-59-6

AUTHOR BIOGRAPHY

Joshua Doder is the author of three novels for children, *A Dog Called Grk, Grk and the Pelotti Gang* and *Grk and the Hot Dog Trail.* He lives in London.